OUR FIRST PICTURE DICTIONARY

BROWN WATSON

(LEICESTER)

Athletics

High Jump

Running

Long
Jump

Shot
Putt

acorn

The Acorn is the nut of the Oak Tree

actor

An Actor is very clever

airport

Planes take-off at an airport

alarm clock

An Alarm clock will wake you up

Aa

anchor

An Anchor stops ships from drifting

ant

An Ant is a busy insect

antler

Antlers are the horns of Deer

anvil

An Anvil is for hammering on

apple

An Apple is a tasty fruit

arch

An Arch is
a curved building

ark

Noah's Ark is
in the Bible

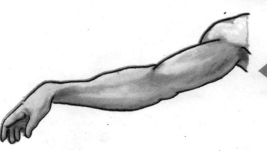

arm

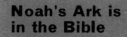

Your arm
helps you
lift objects

arrow

An Arrow is
fired from a bow

axe

An Axe
chops wood

Beach

Cliffs

Lighthouse

yacht

Sand
Dunes

Rocks

Bb

bag

A Bag is used to carry things

ball

A Ball is a sphere

balloon

A Balloon is blown up and tied

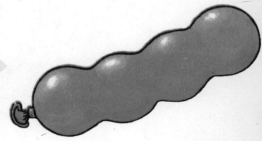

banana

Bananas grow in bunches

Bb

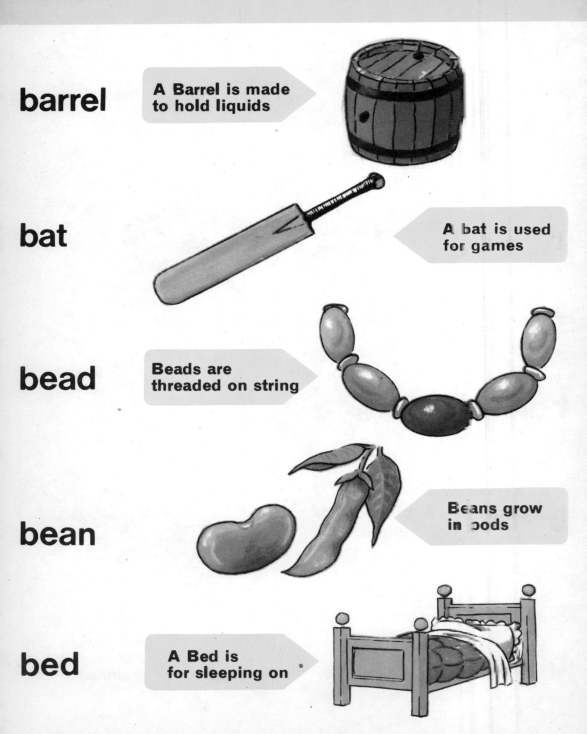

barrel — A Barrel is made to hold liquids

bat — A bat is used for games

bead — Beads are threaded on string

bean — Beans grow in pods

bed — A Bed is for sleeping on

Bb

beetroot

The Beetroot grows in the ground

bell

A Bell rings at churches

black

Black is a colour

black-bird

The blackbird sings sweetly

black-berry

Blackberries grow in country hedgerows

Bb

blue Blue is a colour

bone  Dogs like to eat a bone

book A Book is to be read

boot  Boots keep your feet dry

bottle Bottles are made from glass

box

A Box is used
to keep things

bread

Bread is cut
from the loaf

bridge

A Bridge crosses
one thing over
another

brown

Brown is
a colour

brush

A Brush is used
for painting

Circus

Trapeze Artists

Clowns

Ring Master

Drum Majorettes

Liberty Horses

Cc

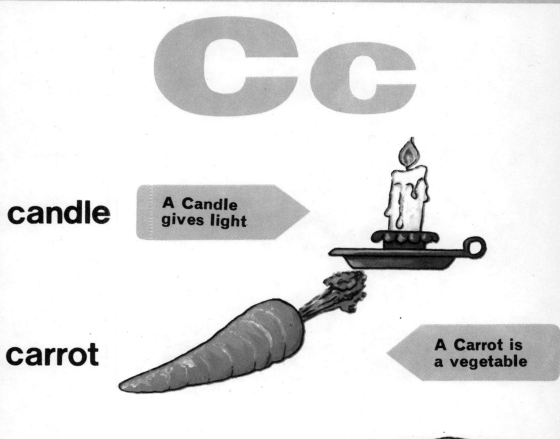

candle   A Candle gives light

carrot   A Carrot is a vegetable

cart   A Cart is a small waggon

castle   A Castle has strong walls

Cc

cat

A Cat is
a pet

caterpillar

A Caterpillar turns
into a butterfly

chair

A Chair is
to sit on

chalks

Chalks are for
writing on
blackboards

cheese

Cheese is made
from milk

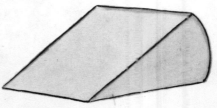

cherries

Cherries grow on trees

chimney

A chimney takes away the smoke

chocolate

Chocolate is nice to eat

chops

Chops are pieces of meat

clock

The clock shows what time it is

Cc

cloud   A Cloud floats high in the sky

coat   A Coat keeps you warm

cobweb   A Cobweb is made by spiders

collar   A Collar is worn round the neck

comb   A Comb is for tidying the hair

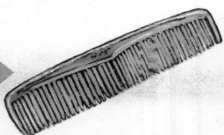

cot

A Cot is
a bed for babies

crab

A Crab lives
on the sea shore

crane

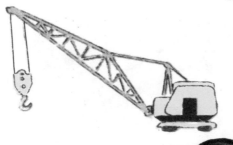

A Crane lifts
heavy objects

crow

A Crow is a big
black bird

cup

A Cup is for
drinking

Dd

Dd

daffodil

A Daffodil is
a pretty flower

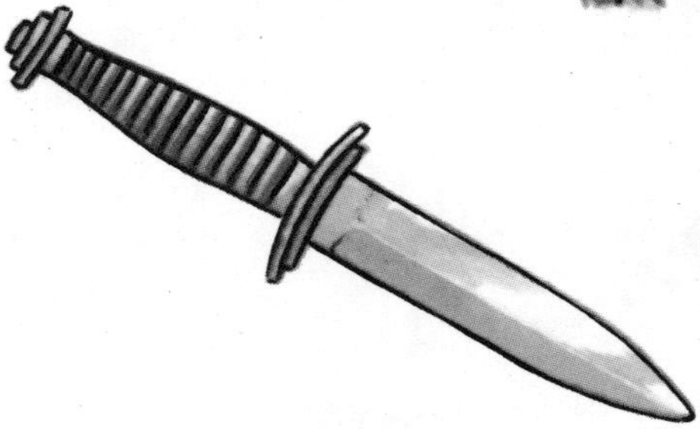

dagger

A Dagger is
very sharp

daisy

A Daisy has
many petals

dam

A Dam stops
water

Dd

dart
A Dart has a sharp point

dates
Dates are good to eat

deer
Deer live in a forest

diamond
A Diamond sparkles

dice
Dice have six sides

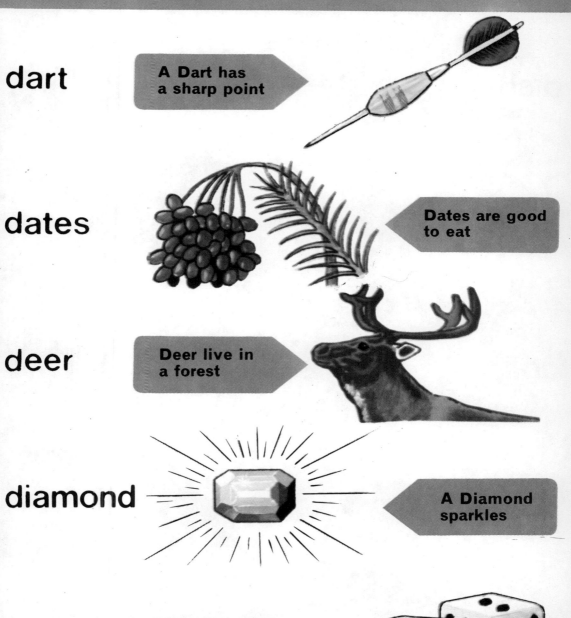

Dd

dish

You eat
off a dish

dog

A dog is
a pet

doll

A doll is
a toy

dolphin

A Dolphin is
a sea mammal

donkey

A Donkey is
a hard working
animal

door — You go through a door

dove — A dove is a tame bird

dress — Girls wear dresses

drum — You beat a drum

duck — Ducks live in the water

Ee

Ee

eagle

An Eagle is
a large bird

ear

An ear is
for hearing with.

easel

The blackboard
rests on an easel

eel

An Eel lives
under water

egg

An Egg comes from a bird

engine

An Engine pulls the carriages

envelope

Letters are posted in an envelope

ewe

A Ewe is a female sheep

eye

An eye is for seeing with

Funfair

Helter
Skelter

Ferris
Wheel

Rifle
Range

Roundabout

Ff

face

The face is the front

fan

A Fan keeps you cool

feather

Birds have feathers

fence

A Fence stops animals straying

Ff

fern

Ferns grow in woodland

fig

A Fig is a fruit

finger

Point with a finger

fir

Fir trees are softwoods

fire

Fire is hot

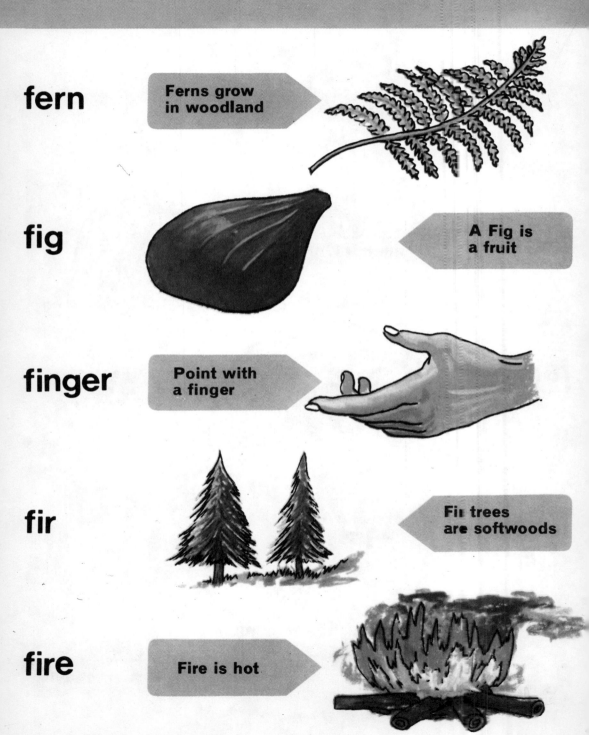

fish

Fish live
in water

flag

Flags fly
from Flagpoles

flask

Flasks keep
liquids hot

flower

Flowers are pretty

flowerpot

Flowers grow
in Flowerpots

Ff

fly

A fly will
spread diseases

flute

Flutes make
pretty music

football

Play games
with a football

forest

Many trees
make a forest

fork

You eat
with a fork

fountain

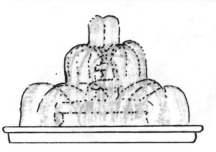

A Fountain is a
display of water

fox

A Fox is
a wild dog

fruit

Fruit is very
good to eat

funnel

A Funnel is a
ship's chimney

fur

Some animals
grow fur

Gg

Gg

garage
A Garage is where you buy petrol

garden

A Garden is where flowers grow

gate
A Gate is an opening in a fence
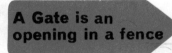

geyser

A Geyser is a hot water spring
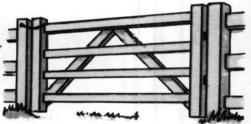

girder

A Girder is a steel brace

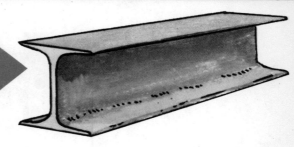

glacier

A Glacier is a river of ice

glass

A Glass is for drinking

glass-house

A Glasshouse is to keep plants warm

gloves

Gloves keep your hands warm

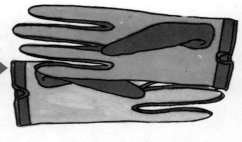

Gg

goblet

A Goblet is a drinking vessel

goldfish

A Goldfish is a pet fish

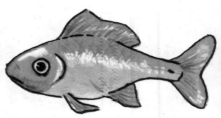

gong

A Gong is beaten to summon people

goose

A Goose is a big bird which hisses

goose-berry

A Gooseberry is a green fruit

gown

A Gown is an expensive dress

grapes

Grapes grow on vines

grass

Grass grows in fields and gardens

green

Green is a colour

gun

This Gun is a revolver

Hh

Hh

ham Ham is a leg of pork

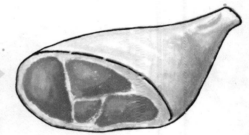

hammer A Hammer is used to hit things

hand A Hand is for grasping

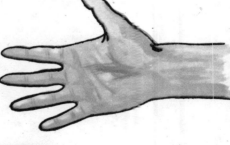

handbag A Handbag is used to carry things

harp

A Harp makes nice music

hat

A Hat is worn on the head

haystack

A Haystack is found in the country

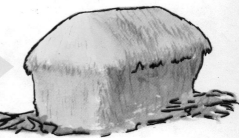

hedge

A Hedge is trimmed to shape

hedgehog

A Hedgehog has sharp spines

Hh

helmet

A Helmet protects your head

hen

A Hen is a farmyard fowl

hill

A Hill is hard to climb!

hinge

A Hinge is used on doors

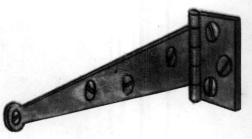

hive

A Hive is where bees live

Hh

hoe

A Hoe is used to till the ground

hook

A Hook holds things up

horn

A Horn makes a loud noise

horse

A Horse is an animal that is ridden

hut

A Hut is where gardening tools are kept

Ii

iceberg

An Iceberg is a danger to shipping

icecream

An Icecream is delicious to eat

iceskates

Iceskates are for moving about on ice

icicles

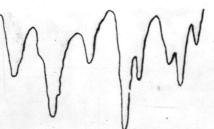

Icicles are cold!

idol

An idol is a statue

igloo

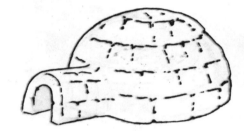

An eskimo lives in an igloo

ink

Ink is used for writing

BLUE INK

inch

An inch is a unit of measurement

insects

Insects are very small creatures with several legs

Ii

iris

An Iris is
a flower

iron

An iron keeps
clothing pressed

island

An island is
surrounded by
water

ivory

Ivory is
the tusks
of Elephants

ivy

Ivy is a plant

Jj

jacket

A Jacket is a piece of clothing

jaguar

A Jaguar is a large wild cat

jam

Jam is made from fruit and sugar

jar

A Jar is a container

Jj

javelin

A Javelin is a throwing spear

jet

A Jet flies very fast

jewellery

Jewellery is very precious

judge

A Judge sentences criminals

jug

A Jug holds drinks

Kk

kangaroo

Kangaroos live
in Australia.

kettle

Water boils
in a kettle

key

A key opens locks

kid

A Kid is
a baby goat

K k

kingfisher A Kingfisher is a pretty bird

kitten A Kitten is a baby cat

knife A Knife is used to cut things

knot A Knot stops ropes from slipping

koala Koala Bears live in trees in Australia

Leaves

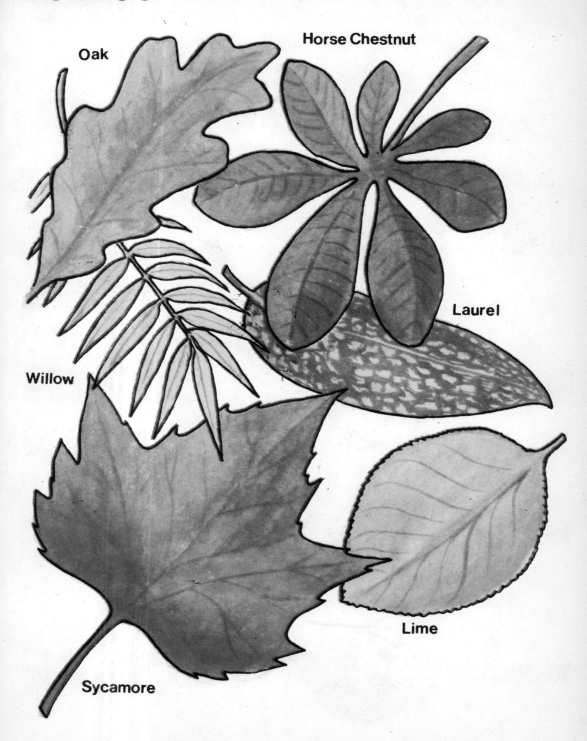

Oak

Horse Chestnut

Laurel

Willow

Lime

Sycamore

Ll

Ll

label

A Label is used to identify objects

ladder

Ladders are climbed

ladle

A Ladle is used to serve soup

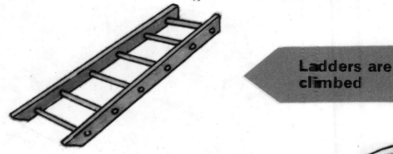

ladybird

A Ladybird is a flying insect

lake

A Lake is water surrounded by land

lance

Knights carry lances

lamb

A Lamb is a baby sheep

lamp

Lamps give light

lasso

A Lasso is used to catch animals

Ll

leek

A Leek is a vegetable

lemon

A Lemon is a citrus fruit

letter

A Letter comes through the post

light

A Light helps you see at night

lighthouse

A Lighthouse warns ships off rocks

lilac

A Lilac is
a flower

lion

A Lion is
the King of Beasts

lime

A Lime is
a citrus fruit

limpet

Limpets live
in the sea

loaf

A Loaf of Bread

Ll

lock

A Lock keeps things secure

log

A Log is a cut up tree

lollypop

A Lollypop is nice to eat

lorry

A Lorry is used to transport goods

luggage

Clothes are packed in luggage

Mm

marbles

Marbles is a popular game

mayor

Mayors are the town leaders

mask

A Mask is used as a disguise

maypole

Maypoles are danced around

Mm

mat

You wipe your feet on a mat

melon

A Melon is a fruit

medal

Medals are given for bravery

mistletoe

Mistletoe grows on Oak trees

mince-pies

Mincepies are eaten at Christmas

mirror

You see yourself in a mirror

mitten

Mittens keep your hands warm

money-box

You keep your money in a money-box

monkey

Monkeys clamber about trees in the jungle

moon

The moon is in the sky at night

Mm

mop

A Mop is used to wipe the floor

mountain

Mountains are very high

mouse

A Mouse is a little animal

music

Music tells us how to play an instrument

mussels

Mussels live in the sea

Nuts

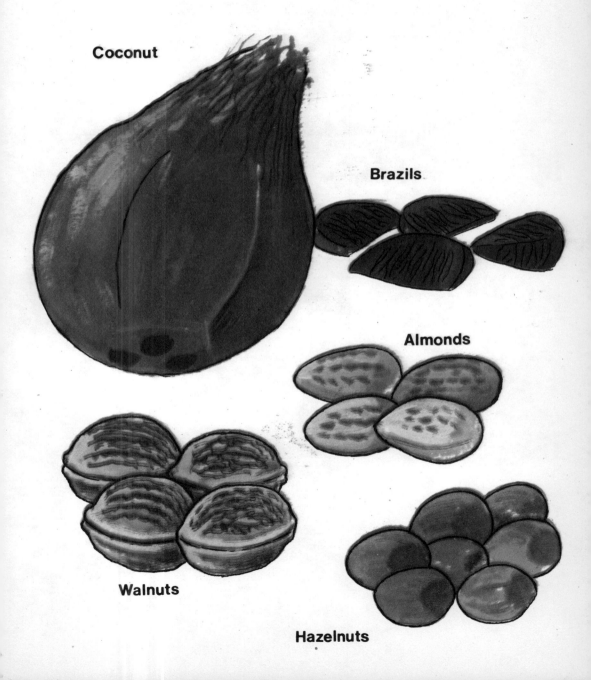

Coconut

Brazils

Almonds

Walnuts

Hazelnuts

Nn

nail

A Nail joins pieces of wood together

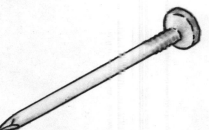

napkin

A Napkin keeps you clean at Dinner

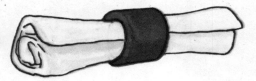

necklace

A Necklace is jewellery worn round the neck

needle

You sew with a needle

nest

Birds live in a nest

net

You catch things in a net

nettle

Nettles are plants that sting

newspaper

Newspapers tell you the news

noon

Noon means twelve o'clock — midday

Nn

north

North is the prime direction

nose

Your Nose is for smelling with

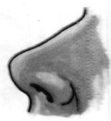

notepad

Notepads are for writing in

nut – cracker

Nutcrackers break open nuts

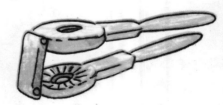

nutmeg

Nutmeg is a spice

O o

oak

Oak is a tree on which acorns grow

oar

You row a boat with an oar

oasis

An Oasis is a pool in the desert

oats

Oats are a cereal from which you make porridge

Oo

ocean

The Ocean is the sea

octopus

An Octopus lives in the sea

oilcan

An oilcan squirts oil

olive

Olives grow on trees

onion

An Onion is a vegetable

opera glasses

Opera glasses make People look larger

orange

Orange is a colour

orange

An Orange is a fruit

organ

An organ plays music

osprey

An Osprey is a bird

Oo

otter

An otter is
an animal that
lives in the water

ouzel

An ouzel is
a bird

owl

An owl is
a night bird

ox

An Ox is a
beast of burden

oyster
catcher

An oyster catcher
is a bird that
eats oysters

Pp

pail

A Pail holds water

paint

Paint is used to make things colourful

GLOSS

pan

You cook food in a pan

parachute

A parachute stops you falling too fast

Pp

parcel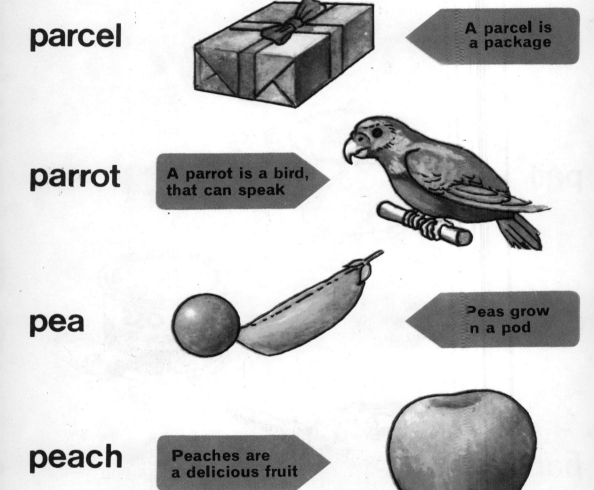

A parcel is a package

parrot

A parrot is a bird, that can speak

pea

Peas grow in a pod

peach

Peaches are a delicious fruit

peanut

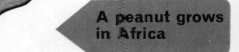

A peanut grows in Africa

Pp

pear

A pear is a fruit

pen

You write with a pen

pencil

You draw with a pencil

piano

A Piano is a musical instrument

pie

A Pie is nice to eat

Pp

pig

A Pig is a farmyard animal

pigeon

A Pigeon is a bird

pillarbox

Letters are posted in a pillarbox

pillow

You rest your head on a pillow

pineapple

A Pineapple is a tropical fruit

Pp

pink

Pink is
a colour

pipe

Tobacco is put
in a pipe

pistol

A pistol is
a small gun

plate

You eat
off a plate

plum

A Plum is
a fruit

Pp

pond

A pond is
a small lake

pony

A pony is
a small horse

poppy

A Poppy is
a flower

pram

A Pram is to
carry babies

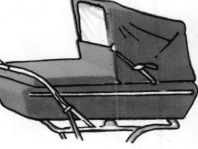

puppy

A Puppy is
a young dog

Qq

Qq

quack

Ducks go quack

quail

A quail is
a wild bird

quarry

Stone comes
from a Quarry

quart

A quart is
two pints

2 PINTS

1 PINT

Qq

quarter

Four quarters make one

quartz

Quartz is a clear crystal

queen

A queen wears a crown

quilt

A quilt is a bedspread

quiver

A quiver is a case for arrows

Rr

rabbit

A rabbit is
a small animal

racket

A racket is
a stringed bat

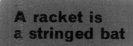

radish

A radish is
a vegetable

rain

Rain falls
from the sky

Rr

rainbow

A rainbow shows many colours

rake

A rake is a garden tool

raspberry

A raspberry is a fruit

rattle

Babies play with rattles

red

Red is a colour

reel

Cotton is
on a reel

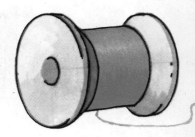

ribbon

A ribbon is worn
in the hair

ring

A ring is worn
on the finger

river

Boats sail
on the river

robot

A robot is a
mechanical man

Rr

roof

A roof covers a house

root

Trees have roots

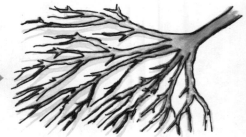

ruin

A ruin is a broken down building

rose

A rose is a pretty flower

rug

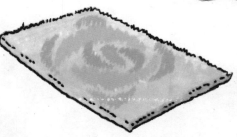

A rug is a small carpet

Ss

safe

Valuables are kept in a safe

sails

Yachts have sails

salmon

Salmon is good to eat

sandals

Sandals are open shoes

sandwich A Sandwich is made of sliced bread

sausage A Sausage is made from meat

saw A Saw is used to cut wood

scissors Scissors are used to cut string

sheep Sheep give us wool

Ss

shell

A Shell is found on the sea shore

ship

Ships sail the seas

shoe

Shoes are worn on the feet

skirt

A Skirt hangs from the waist

sledge

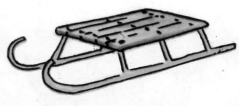

A Sledge runs over snow

slipper

Slippers keep your feet warm

snail

The snail lives in a shell

snake

A Snake crawls along the ground

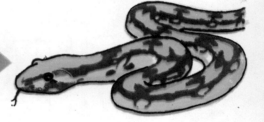

soap

Soap keeps you clean

socks

Socks are short stockings

Ss

spade

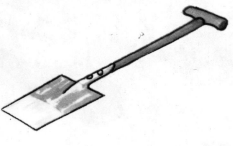

A Spade is for digging the garden

stamp

You put stamps on envelopes

star

A Star has five points

stone

A stone is hard and heavy

sun

The sun is hot

Tt

table

You sit at a table to eat

tack

A tack pins things to a wall

tap

Water comes from a tap

teapot

Tea is made in a teapot

Tt

teddybear

A Teddybear is a toy bear

telephone

You can talk to people on a telephone

television

Television brings pictures to you

tent

A Tent is used for camping

thistle

A Thistle has sharp prickles

thread

Clothes are sewn with thread

tie

A Tie is worn round the neck

tiger

A Tiger is a large wild cat

toad

A Toad lives by water

toadstool

Toadstools are poisonous

T t

tomato

A Tomato is red

tooth

A tooth helps you to chew your food properly

tower

A Tower is a tall building

train

A Train takes you on a journey

tree

A Tree has leaves

trumpet A Trumpet is a musical instrument

turban A Turban is worn on the head

turkey A Turkey is a large farmyard fowl

turtle A Turtle lives in the ocean

tyre A tyre is made from rubber

Uu

Uu

ukelele

A Ukelele is
a small guitar

umbrella

An Umbrella keeps
off rain

uniform

Soldiers wear
a uniform

urn

An urn holds water

V v

vacuum cleaner

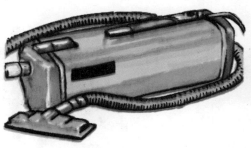

A Vacuum cleaner sucks up dirt

vegetables

Vegetables are good to eat

violin

A violin is a musical instrument

violet

A Violet is a pretty flower

W w

W w

waggon

A Waggon is seen on the farm

wallaby

A Wallaby is a small kangaroo

watch

A Watch shows the time

water

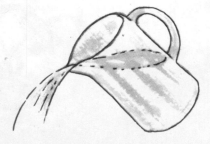

Water is vital to life

waterfall Water falling in a stream

watermill A Watermill is driven by water

weasel A Weasel is a small animal

well There is water in a well

whale The whale is the largest animal and lives in the sea

W w

wheel

A wheel goes round and round

whistle

Is a musical instrument

windmill

Windmills can be seen in Holland

window

A window lets in the light

witch

A Witch is ugly

wolf

A Wolf is a wild dangerous animal

wren

A small song bird

xylophone

A Xylophone is a musical instrument

xmas tree

You hang lights and decorations on a Christmas Tree

Y y

Y y

yacht

A Yacht is a boat with sails

yard

A measure of length

yarn

Yarn is thread which can be used for knitting

yellow

Yellow is a colour

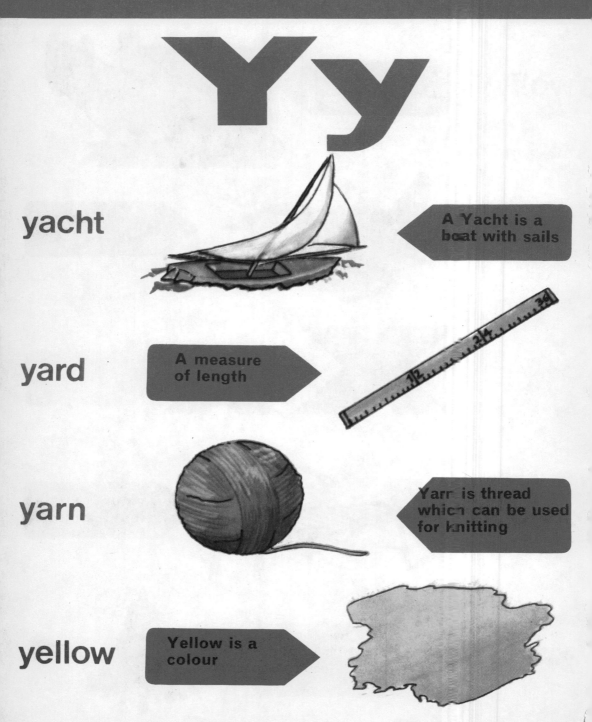

Zz

zebra

A Zebra has black and white stripes

zero

Zero is the figure 0

zig-zag

Zig-zag is a crooked line

zip

Zips are used to keep clothes together

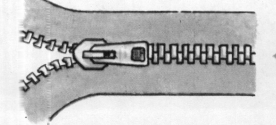